OURHOUSE.COM

Presents

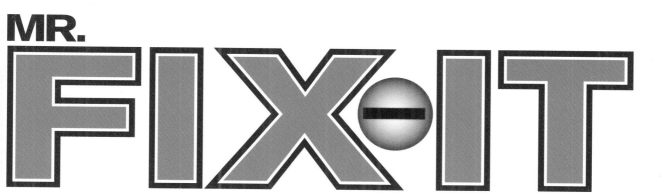

MR.

FIX-IT

OURHOUSE.COM

Chances are, if you're holding this book in your hands, you want guidance. You need answers. Simple and straightforward.

That's why we created a place where everything comes together. A place where you can learn to silence a leaky faucet, shop for a ceiling fan, and determine the tools you'll need to hang a mailbox —all in one visit—www.ourhouse.com.

Home improvement projects can be frustrating, that's why OurHouse.com brings you Lou Manfredini. Like your handy neighbor, Lou knows glue works better than gum, plaster's tougher than drywall and vinegar cleans hardwood floors. He's here to lend a hammer and a reassuring pat on the back.

He provides tips and stories on everything —from choosing the right smoke alarm to cleaning out your gutters. He also answers questions in our Online Community.

We make home improvement easy. So whether you're just starting a project, or in the middle of one— don't leave your house.

Just visit ours.

DESIGNED AND PRODUCED BY

RARE AIR MEDIA
1711 North Paulina, Suite 311, Chicago, Illinois 60622

Written by Lou Manfredini and edited by Kathy Neumeyer
Illustrations by Karen Favakeh

Special Thanks
At Rare Air Media:
Creative: John Vieceli, Seth Guge
Production: Dennis Carlson, Melinda Fry
Promotion: Lisa Butler, Jim Carlton
Sales: Heidi Knack
Executive Staff: Mark Vancil, Jim Forni

At OurHouse.com:
Gary Briggs, Tom Tresser, Natalie True

Rare Air books may be purchased for educational, business, or sales promotional use.
For information please contact Jim Forni at Rare Air Media (773) 342-5180.

First Edition
Library of Congress Cataloging-in-publication Data is available from the Publisher.
ISBN 1-892866-15-3
Printed in the United States of America.
99 00 01 02 RA 10 9 8 7 6 5 4 3 2 1

Table of Contents

Introduction

Since 1995, I have spent Saturday mornings answering home repair and renovation questions from listeners who tune into the "Mr. Fix-It" show on WGN Radio 720 AM in Chicago. As a side job, I also own a development company that constructs rental properties and single family custom homes. This has been my "hobby" for the past fourteen years.

I have lost count how often a listener calls the show asking, "I heard you talk about this last month, and now I'm having the same problem . . . can you explain it again?" And as a builder, I too, confront the same issues over and over, just like my listeners. I began to see a trend. I realized that I could quite easily compile a list of the most commonly asked questions that I hear from my listeners and clients, not to mention the barrage of questions from family, friends and neighbors. The list evolved into this book.

I wanted to create a handy reference book that would address the most common problems, not everything under the sun—something selective, not comprehensive, and written with the assumption that the reader is not a home repair expert. I have written this book for new homeowners and home repair novices, but it will be helpful to veteran handy people as well. I have included specific topics detailing simple home repair remedies, as well as complex, contracted projects.

Introduction

Many of my listeners ask for leads on reliable, skilled contractors. (And we all know how hard it is to find good help these days!) That is why I included topics detailing specific questions to ask a contractor, electrician or plumber. I also included a chapter on "How to Choose a Contractor." In addition, many listeners need advice about which products to use when doing home repairs, or what to buy when replacing a major appliance. So I've included topics that discuss which products I recommend from brass cleaners to cold water heaters. I've also added an appendix that lists the products I recommend throughout the book. With more than fourteen years experience in this industry, I've tried almost every product out there. Every product I recommend is one that I use regularly in the homes I build and in my own home.

As I write this book, I realize that the book has written itself. I've just extrapolated the questions I hear repeatedly from my listeners and clients, friends and family. I hope you find this home improvement advice to be entertaining, cost-saving and above all, useful.

Lou Manfredini

CHAP

TER·1

Interior Repairs

Two nails keep popping out through the drywall in my living room ceiling. They reappear despite my attempts to re-hammer them and re-patch the ceiling. Is there anything I can do short of replacing that piece of drywall?

Have I got a fix for you! Install two drywall screws on either side of the nails–approximately four inches away from each nail (Figure 1). Next, remove the nasty, popping nails. The screws will not pop. Patch the area with some spackling compound, paint and be happy.

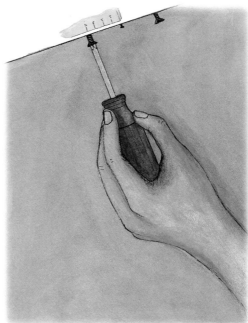

Figure 1

The three-year-old, ceramic tile in my bathroom has one cracked piece in the middle of the floor. How can a do-it-yourselfer like me, fix this?

How about a nice bath mat? Just kidding. First, remove all of the grout that surrounds the broken tile, using either a grout scraping tool or a linoleum knife. Next, whack the tile with a hammer breaking it into little pieces. Remove the tile and clean the spot so it is smooth and dust–free. Apply tile adhesive and affix the new tile. Allow it to set for 24 hours, then re-grout the tile to match. Now treat yourself to something, like that new bath mat.

In the center of my carpeting there is a spot about the size of a baseball. I've tried all kinds of cleaning methods and it won't budge. What can I do?

Put a small coffee saucer face-down over the spot. Make sure that the saucer is larger than the stain. Cut around the plate with a sharp knife, careful not to cut through the carpet pad (Figure 2). Remove and save the unwanted piece of carpet. Next, from a concealed spot, perhaps under an entertainment center or sofa, repeat this process. Use carpet tacks to install the new piece, then tack the stained piece under the couch. Once in place, only you will know it's there.

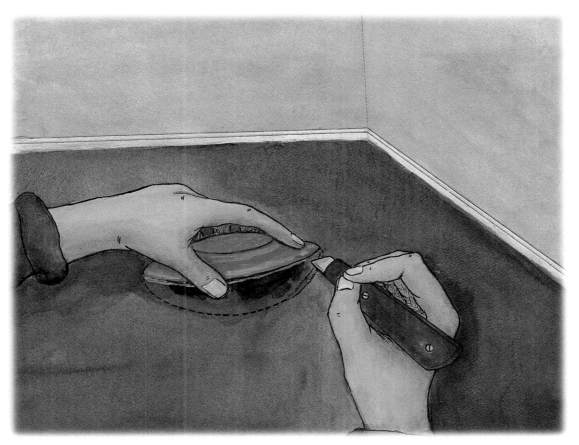

Figure 2

Occasionally, water seeps through hairline cracks in my basement walls. Can I repair it myself or do I need to call a professional?

If the seepage is only occasional, try fixing it yourself using a concrete epoxy kit.

Since the water is not rushing in your basement, the epoxy should seal the leak.

At ten to twenty dollars a tube, it's worth a try.

There is a crack in my basement's foundation about three feet away from my sump pump pit. Every time it rains water flows in through this crack. Can I fix it with a concrete epoxy sealant or do I need to seal it from the outside?

The epoxy will not work under these conditions. It does work well when there is seepage and the floor is only damp. You can do one of two things. First, you can dig down on the outside to expose the foundation wall and seal it, which is the preferred way because it works best. But it requires a lot of hard labor, or money if you don't do it yourself. Or, you can cut a little trough in the concrete floor toward the sump pump. Use a circular saw with a concrete blade to cut a groove in the floor. This creates a channel for the water and guides it right into the sump pump pit. Then, put the epoxy in the vertical crack to slow the leakage.

Water is seeping from my chimney's clean out door. During the past thirty-one years, this has happened only a few times after a severe rain or snow storm. Now, water leaks out regardless of the weather. I recently replaced my old furnace with a new, 80-plus efficiency model. Is there any correlation between this seepage and my new furnace? How can I stop it?

Your seepage is most likely caused by condensation from the furnace. Make sure that your chimney has a chimney liner. Because these new, fancy furnaces are so efficient, they don't lose as much heat or energy. With the 80-plus efficiency models, the flue feeds right into your chimney. As a result, there's not enough heat in that old, brick chimney to draft out the spent gases. These trapped gases create condensation, and may also cause carbon monoxide backup. Therefore, you must install a chimney liner to regulate these gases when upgrading to an 80-plus efficiency furnace. In fact, it is required in most cities and villages. Talk to your heating contractor. Also, make sure that the chimney has a chimney cap.

I am going to install ceramic tile on my bathroom floor. Currently the bathroom has a 14-year-old, sheet good, linoleum floor. Do I need to pull up the existing floor before laying the ceramic? I spoke to one contractor who said to install the ceramic tile over the original floor because the sheet good may contain asbestos. Is this true?

First of all, don't hire that contractor! There is no asbestos in a 14-year-old, linoleum sheet good. Asbestos is usually found in tiles from the 1940's or 1950's. Now as a rule of thumb, never put a finished floor over another finished floor. The only exception is with an old mud-set ceramic floor—the little mosaic tiles that were popular in the 1950's and 1960's. A mud-set floor is a very hard surface and when properly prepared is a great base for new ceramic. As for your linoleum, take it out. Once you remove it, install a stone-based fiberboard over the subfloor. I recommend a DuraRock® fiberboard.

My house is sixteen-years-old. Recently, I've noticed stains across the ceilings and around the top of the walls (in every room beneath attic space). The stains are evenly spaced and occur where the attic rafters cross the ceiling. They won't wash off, how can I get rid of them?

It sounds like you don't have adequate ventilation up in your attic space which is causing excessive moisture. Those ceiling joists are absorbing the moisture, and because the rooms below the attic are heated, this moisture is wicking through the wood and staining the ceiling. There are a few things that you need to do. First, make sure that you have an adequate number of soffit vents above the overhangs of the house. If you cannot feel cold air coming through the vents, then you're not getting enough ventilation. Then, make sure that the insulation is not jammed up in the crotch of the roof—the area between the soffit and the roof (Figure 3). Finally, make sure that you have enough roof vents, either the continuous ridge vents or the mushroom vents. (One mushroom vent is good for about 100 square feet of attic - or one vent per 10 x 10 foot area). If you have any exhaust fans, make sure that they are vented out of the attic space and not just dumping into the attic space. After all these items check out and you can say "this is one well-ventilated attic space," buy a gallon of Killz® Total One and spot prime each of those ceiling rafters. Then, repaint the ceiling.

Figure 3

• airflow • insulation blocking soffit vent
• continuous soffit vents with correct insulation installation • baffles direct airflow

I am having trouble removing wallpaper from my bedroom walls. Do you have suggestions for someone who can't afford hired help?

Run to the paint store and buy a wallpaper wheel and a bottle of DIF® Wallpaper Stripper by Zinsser. Available in liquid and gel formulations, this is about the best darn wallpaper stripper I've ever seen. I like the gel because it adheres well to the wall. First, use the wallpaper wheel to perforate the paper, then apply the DIF® according to package instructions. Once it dries, you'll be able to scrape that wallpaper right off, I promise.

What is your opinion about these new, laminate floors that are on the market?

I prefer these floors to vinyl tile or sheet goods. However they are more expensive. Many styles currently have finishes that resemble wood, but when you walk on them they can feel spongy because they lie on top of the floor like a carpet. I think that if you want a floor that looks like wood, then you should install a real wood floor. It costs less, and is easy to repair.

The hardwood floors in my house squeak like crazy! How can I stop this short of divorcing my early-rising husband?

My wife complains about this in our house. I try to convince her that this is part of the charm of an old home, but she knows I'm full of it. Most hardwood floors are installed over wood sleepers (Figure 4). The weight of someone walking across the floor causes the sleepers and subfloor to shift and, as a result, squeak. Spread some talcum powder over the area that squeaks. Then place a block of wood, like a small piece of 2x4, over that area and hammer the block. Use a baby sledgehammer or some heavy hammer to whack the block of wood. This should reset some of the nails holding the hardwood in place and shake some of that talc into the grooves of the floor. The talc will keep the wood from rubbing together. Your marriage is saved! But realize, now it's going to be hard to hear that early-riser when he tries sneaking in after a late night of poker.

Figure 4

The paint on my bathroom ceiling keeps peeling. I've repainted it three times in the last two years and I'm at my wit's end! Can you help?

You must have a heck of wit, because I would have given up after the second time! It sounds like what you really need is an exhaust fan to get rid of all the moisture in the bathroom. If that is not possible (or even if it is), here is how you can stop the peeling paint. Scrape all the loose paint, and then sand the ceiling to feather the edges between the coats of paint. Next, prime the entire ceiling with B-I-N® Primer Sealer, this will prepare the surface and keep the paint from peeling. Finally, paint the surface with Perma-White Mildew-Proof Bathroom Paint® by Zinsser. Any good paint store will carry these products. Now gather your wits, and take a nice, long shower.

I am going to remodel my kitchen.
Can you recommend a good counter top?

When it comes to buying counter tops, your main consideration is how much you want to spend. We all have seen laminate counter tops (Formica®), and the choices of color and style are really quite good these days. The average cost of a laminate top is around $30.00 per running foot. Laminates look good and are quite durable, but they do scratch and can fade over time. So you must be careful how you treat them. Natural stone counter tops, like granite or marble, are a great choice from a design perspective. There is nothing that looks quite as good as a granite counter. There is also nothing quite as expensive. The average price for these tops is around $140.00 per running foot. (That laminate top is looking better and better!) The down side is that the stone can stain and chip, but it can be repaired by a professional with the right tools. Stone is probably not a practical choice if you have small children. My personal favorite is Corian®. It costs about the same as natural stone, but it does not stain, it is easy to keep clean, it won't chip or fade, and it looks great. Some Corian® styles even have the look of natural stone.

*I am going to refinish the hardwood
floor in my kitchen. What is the best finish
to use? With four children, I expect a lot of
traffic in that room. Once it is completed,
how can I keep it clean?*

With that many in the house, it sounds like you could use a few stop signs. The best finish in my opinion (and since it's my book I can give it) are the new water-based wood floor finishes. These are durable, non-fading, and have a limited odor so you can live through the process. The best one on the market is Street Shoe®. You can choose from several different gloss options, most people prefer the semi-gloss. To clean them, I use Murphys Oil Soap®, and I really do the floors! I wash with a damp cloth and follow with a dry cloth.

I want to paint the front of my old,
wood kitchen cabinets. The doors are in good shape,
but the finish is a little dingy.
What kind of preparation is required for this job?
Can you recommend a good paint to use?

You can easily spruce up those old cabinets for just a few dollars and in just a few days. First and most important, clean the cabinets thoroughly. Use a course sand paper to rough up the surface and remove any glossy finish from the face of the doors and the box. Then, sand the cabinets lightly with a fine sandpaper. I like using a sanding sponge because it easily reaches into small crevices. Once sanded, wipe down the fronts with some mineral spirits and a rag. Then, prime the entire surface using Bulls Eye® 1-2-3 Primer Sealer by Zinsser. (I recommend products from this company so often that I should be the poster child for Zinsser). When priming, make sure you keep your strokes even and that there's no buildup of primer near the corners. Let dry about two hours. Then, lightly sand the fronts with a fine sand paper to blend the primer. Now, paint your cabinets using a semi-gloss or high-gloss paint. I recommend using an oil-based paint on cabinets. It requires several coats to get a nice, deep finish, but the surface will outlast a water-based paint at least three to one. Remember, a good paint brush can make a big difference, so spend a few extra pennies and invest in a high quality brush.

My bedroom door hits the top of the doorjamb.
Someone told me to sand the top of the door.
Will this fix it? How do I do it?

Doors tend to get out of whack as a home settles, a trick is to reset or remortise the door's hinges. With the door closed, inspect the gap between the door and the frame. In a perfect world, it should be equal—about 1/8 of an inch—for both vertical gaps and the horizontal gap at the top. In old homes this gap is almost never uniform. In your case, the top of the door just opposite the hinge is hitting the doorjamb. Remove the bottom hinge from the jamb (not the door). Using a sharp chisel, scrape away about 1/8 of an inch of the jamb to recess the hinge. (See Figure 5). Use the palm of your hand instead of a hammer to hit the chisel, it will give you more control. Now, reinstall the hinge, and open and close the door to your heart's content. This method usually solves sagging doors in a house and is better than sanding or planing a door, because if you're not really accurate, your door will look like it belongs in a fun house at the circus.

Figure 5

My basement has really ugly paneling.
Will it look better if I paint it?
What materials should I use?

Refer to question 15 about painting your kitchen cabinets. You use the same method to paint your paneling. This is a great way to brighten up a room. This look is really popular right now. So if you need ideas, check out any decorating magazine.

*There is a crack in my drywall that will not go away.
Every year I fill it, sand it, prime it and paint it,
but it keeps coming back. How can I get rid
of this problem once and for all?*

You could move? All right, maybe not. You're not going to like this answer, but it will solve your problem. Chances are this area is a stress point in your home, and movement in your home will always open it up. Locate the studs that are at least sixteen inches away from both sides of the crack. Then, cut out the drywall, and create a rectangle hole that is larger than the length of the crack—about a foot longer on both sides (Figure 6). Install a new piece of drywall, and fasten it using drywall screws. Then, apply joint tape and joint compound, sand, and paint. You just worked your tail off, but it's the last time you have to deal with that crack.

Figure 6

ceiling joist • cutaway view • stud

I am going to paint my dining room dark blue. Are there any special preparations required before I paint my walls with such a dark color?

Dark colors have become really popular. The real key is to begin with a clean and smooth wall, then cover it with at least four coats of paint. After you clean the wall, sand and prime it using an acrylic-based primer. Ask your paint dealer to add a little tint to the primer so the finish paint covers better. Take your time painting, the more coats you apply, the deeper the finish will appear on the wall.

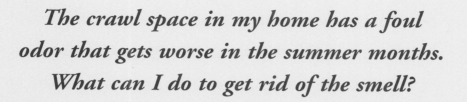

The crawl space in my home has a foul odor that gets worse in the summer months. What can I do to get rid of the smell?

My guess is that the space is not properly ventilated. First, see if there is moisture seeping in from somewhere such as a crack in the foundation, or a down spout dumping water too close to the foundation. If this checks out, make sure you have foundation vents at each end of your home. These allow air to flow through the space. You can also install exhaust fans that will help remove any moisture and fumes. Finally, a properly prepared crawl space contains a layer of plastic that covers the ground dirt, and a layer of gravel that covers the plastic. If you do not have this plastic layer, you should install it.

My home has an unfinished, walk-up attic.
In the summer it gets so hot that it heats up
the entire second floor. I usually ventilate that space
by putting a fan in one window and opening another
window across the room. Is there something more
permanent I can do that will work better?

Sure, you need an attic fan that is cut through the roof and set up with a thermostat.

Broan Manufacturing Co. makes a very quiet fan with a self-controlled thermostat.

When it gets hot up there, the fan starts automatically until the temperature cools down.

However if you're not too handy, you'll need to hire a couple of professionals to do the

job—a roofer to install the fan, and an electrician to wire it up. I have one in my home,

and it works great.

*My kids have created some of their best art work
on my dining room walls using crayons and markers.
How do I clean it? To combat future wall murals,
is there a paint I can use that is easy to clean?*

Those little buggers! Clean off as much as you can using acetone and a sponge. Then,

spot prime the walls using Bulls Eye® 1-2-3 Primer Sealer by Zinsser. Now you can repaint.

Use a paint with an eggshell (enamel) finish. It is harder and less shiny than a semi-gloss,

which in turn is easy to clean. Nothing will combat marker drawings on your wall, but

you'll have a fighting chance against the crayons. Just think, years from now you'll be

laughing about this.

My old wood windows always stick in the summertime. I put baby powder in the track which seems to correct the problem, but only temporarily. How can I keep them from jamming for good?

I am surprised that the baby powder worked at all, it is not a very good lubricant. But I bet your windows smell good! Wood is constantly expanding and contracting, especially in the extreme temperatures of summer and winter. Combine that with rain and humidity and you've got a "sticky" situation on your hands, especially if the window frames are painted. To keep them from jamming, remove the sash from the window frame and sand down the vertical portions of the sash. If you cannot remove the sashes, take a block of wood that fits just inside the vertical jamb of the window and tap it with a hammer (Figure 7). This will widen the opening and allow the window to open and close with ease.

Figure 7

When I turn on my ceiling fan, it wobbles like crazy. Is there anything I can do to stop this?

Most ceiling fans come with a balancing kit. If you didn't know what it was when you bought your fan, you might have thrown it away. Most hardware stores or home centers sell these kits. Each contains a small white clip that resembles a clothespin and a self-adhesive lead weight. Attach the clip to one blade and turn on the fan. Continue this process, placing the clip onto each blade, until you locate the wobble. Now, attach the lead weight to the back of the blade.

My upstairs bathroom has an awful
lot of mildew (my kids take these long, hot showers).
Is there anything I can do to remove it and prevent
mold from returning, short of getting rid of my kids?

Think of all the money you could save on college tuition! You did not mention if you have an exhaust fan. If not, have one installed. Buy a fan that has a cubic feet per minute (cfm) rating of 100, which means that it exhausts the air at a rate of 100 cfm. Also, to ensure quiet operation select a fan with a low sone rating. Use the fan after each shower and run it a minimum of thirty minutes. Finally, repaint the bathroom with a mildew proof paint. Better yet, make your kids repaint it. I recommend Perma-White Mildew-Proof Bathroom Paint® by Zinsser.

The tile grout in my bathroom shower is moldy and crumbling in some spots. Do I need to replace all the grout or can I just clean some spots and replace others? How do I do it?

If the tile itself is in good shape, not faded or cracked, and the wall behind the tile is not spongy, then yes you can repair the grout in those areas. The key here is to thoroughly remove all of the old grout. But let me warn you, after you finish this job your forearms will be aching. Use either a grout scraping tool or a linoleum knife to scrape out the old grout all the way down to the backing. Then vacuum out any dust (Figure 8). Once it is cleaned out and dry, you can apply the new grout. I use a product manufactured by TEC it is available in a ton of colors and it works great. Mix according to the package directions and apply it with a grout float (it looks like a rectangular iron). Make sure you wipe off the excess grout from the face of the tile before it completely drys, this will save you from more scrubbing (and aching arms) later.

Figure 8

CHAP

TER•2

Exterior Repairs

Every winter I battle with ice dams that form on my roof and in my gutters. Though I clean the gutters every fall, the ice returns each winter. How can I get rid of the ice?

You know what they say about ice dams? They wouldn't be so bad if it wasn't for all that damn ice! But seriously, the key to eliminating ice buildup is to maintain the same temperature between your roof and the air outside. To do this, keep your attic well-ventilated. Continuous soffit vents and continuous ridge vents enable air to flow into the attic and then circulate out the top of the roof (Figure 9). Also, be sure that there is no insulation stuck in the crotch of the roof rafter. This can block air flow into the soffit vents. Also make sure your ceiling insulation has an r25 rating.

• airflow • insulation • continuous soffit vents • **continuous ridge vents** • baffles

Figure 9

My gutters have a few leaks at the seams and in the corners. I've tried patching them with tar, but they still leak. What can I do?

Don't you just hate that? This is the last time you will fix it. Buy a couple of tubes of gutter sealant such as NPC Solar Seal® from a siding or gutter supply company. (Contractors use this product to install new, seamless gutters.) Carefully wash the area, then dry it using a blow dryer or heat gun. Use a caulk gun to apply the gutter sealant, forcing the compound into and over the seam (Figure 10). Make sure that the gutter remains dry overnight.

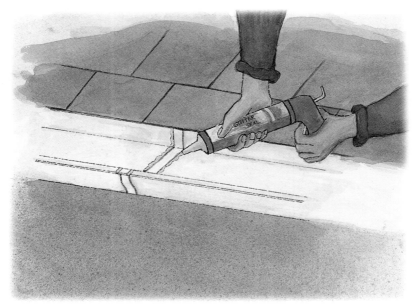

Figure 10

My vinyl siding is cracked right next to my front door. Now the siding suppliers say that the color has been discontinued. I have a small section of the original siding in my garage, can I use this piece to repair it?

There are two ways to attack this problem–repair or replace the broken piece. Either way, you need a zip tool to separate the siding from the middle of the wall. Just follow the directions on the package; zip tools are easy to use. To repair the siding, first remove the cracked segment (Figure 11), then clean the back with a PVC cleaner. Cut a section from the unused piece of siding that is larger than the crack. Attach it to the backside of the broken piece using a PVC cement. Allow it to dry approximately two minutes and then reinstall the siding. To replace the cracked siding, remove a different segment from an inconspicuous area, say the side of the garage. Just make sure that the replacement piece is larger than the broken piece. Install the new section by the front door and the cracked one on the garage. Who cares about a little crack there?

Figure 11

cutaway view • seem or cut • crack

My house has old, aluminum siding that is very faded and chalky. Do I have to re-side my house, or can I paint it?

Yes, you can paint it. Realizing that once you do, the siding is no longer maintenance-free. There are several good products on the market made specifically for aluminum siding. I typically use the aluminum siding paint manufactured by Benjamin Moore®. The key to this job is the preparation. I recommend using a power washer to clean the siding. Not only is it great for scouring that chalky siding, but it's fun to use. You can rent one from your local builder's supply center. Get one with a pressure of at least 1500 psi (pounds per square inch). Just be careful. If you get too close, the high water pressure can poke a hole in the siding. Once it is clean and dry, undercoat with a siding primer such as Killz® Total One. Now, you are ready to paint. Now remember, in a few years you may have to touch up or repaint as you do with wood siding.

Some new, brick homes are under construction in my neighborhood. I noticed that at first the builders put up wooden walls. Now they are laying brick around those walls. Is that really how a brick home is built?

Actually that is a wood frame house with brick siding, or a face brick home. Face brick homes have been around for a long time, and they are a great way to make a home more solid and appear more expensive for the least amount of cost. If you are building a home and are thinking of brick, I would suggest you look into a solid masonry home. Yes it costs more, but that added cost adds value that will last forever. Besides, a true masonry home feels like nothing else. You will feel it the first time you slam the front door after your wife kicks you out. You'll think, man that's a solid home, I wish she'd let me back in!

My concrete stoop is sagging about four inches on one corner. What can I do?

Mudjacking or slabjacking is a technique that has been around for a long time, and will work well in this situation. Using this procedure, a contractor simply pumps a grout-like, cement solution under your stoop until it is level (Figure 12). Once the cement cures, it provides a very even and solid base. Plus, it costs about half the price of putting in a new stoop.

grout entrance • grout

Figure 12

My three-year-old deck is filthy. My friend suggested that I use one of those exterior wood cleaning products. There are so many formulas to choose from, which one should I use? Do these products even work?

They surely do! I recommend Wolman® Deck Rejuvenator. It is available in two formulas —one for treated lumber and one for cedar and redwood. Apply with a brush roller or sprayer. Scrub the treated wood using a bristle brush and a lot of elbow grease. Once you have removed all the dirt and grime, apply a good wood preservative. I recommend products from Cabot® Stains and Penofin®. Wood preservatives keep your deck looking good for years

The top of my front door scrapes whenever I use it, making it difficult to open or close. Someone told me to plane down the top, is that the right thing to do?

That is one solution, but I'll offer you another. Remove the bottom hinge from the door. Use a chisel to shave a thin layer from the area behind the hinge (See Figure 13). A hinge normally lies recessed in the door jamb. This technique adds a slight recess to the hinge and changes the position of the door. This method works well for interior doors as well. (See question #16).

Figure 13

My exterior, brass light fixtures look very lackluster. What can I do to polish them and prevent them from dulling in the future?

Because of the environment, brass tends to dull and tarnish. But you can slow this effect. Use a product called Brasso® (it's the stuff your Mom used for cleaning and it works great) to polish and shine your fixtures. Next, apply three coats of a clear lacquer spray that contains a UV blocker. The lacquer slows the climate's detrimental effects. You must still clean your fixtures, but now your brass will have a dazzling shine for two or three years.

I've been getting estimates from contractors to tuckpoint my house. One contractor claims that he must grind out the old, loose mortar, wash the walls, and then install new mortar. Another says that he needs only to wash the walls and install the new mortar. The second contractor's price is much lower, but I want to make sure that the job is done right. Which method should I choose?

I agree with the first contractor. This renovation will yield the most comprehensive and enduring results. Though many contractors use a pressure washer to clean the brick and remove any loose mortar that may fall, this is not enough. The key to tuckpointing is to remove as much mortar as possible to create a uniform cavity for the new mortar (Figure 14). Provided this first contractor is well recommended and can supply references, spend the extra money. You'll be happier with the results. It's just like everything else in life, you get what you pay for.

Figure 14

Eight years ago, I sealed my garage floor with a no-color sealer. Now I'd like to paint the floor. Can you recommend any paints to use, or should I just reseal it?

I do not recommend that you paint your garage floor. Though garage paints provide a nice finish, they inevitably will peel. The paint cannot withstand the forces of friction caused by the car's weight and motion. Combine this with salt, oil and dirt, and your beautiful floor doesn't stand a chance. If you are willing to spend a little more money, you can hire a contractor to seal your floor with a concrete epoxy coating. The epoxy is impervious to oil and salt, so it cleans up well and won't tear apart. This product comes with a great warranty and can be used on exterior stoops and sidewalks. If you still want to reseal the surface, I recommend that you buy a commercial grade sealer with absorbent properties. You probably noticed when you sealed your floor it became very slick. This occurs because your very porous garage floor has a very smooth finish to keep it from absorbing too much moisture. Mix the sealer with silica sand so you're not falling on your keester.

Water seeps out of my brick chimney
when there is a heavy rain. My friend told
me that the chimney needs a chimney cap,
but I don't even know the source of the leak.
What should I do?

If the leak only happens when there is a heavy rain, then a chimney cap is a good place to start. I'd also check the flashing—the weatherproofing between where the roof meets the chimney. This flashing can pull away from the brick and cause water seepage (Figure 15). Finally, check the condition of the brick. If you see a lot of gaps in the mortar at the top of the chimney, it may be time to have that old thing tuckpointed and sealed. This should keep you busy for a while. Good luck.

Figure 15

I want to paint my house, should I use an oil-based or a water-based paint?

If you had asked me this about five years ago, I would have recommended an oil-based paint. Today, an oil-based paint still works great, but I recommend using a water-based (acrylic) paint. Water-based paints have come so far in the past several years. They not only look good and cleanup easily, but they are friendly to the environment. As a home builder, I always struggle with the fact that I use so many natural resources to do my job. Any chance I have to do something environmentally friendly, I'll do it. So paint your house, stand back and admire how beautiful it looks, and then go hug a tree.

I want to replace my windows, but I am not sure whether to buy them with vinyl or wood frames. I plan to stain the frames on the inside, while I want to do little or no work on the outside. Do you have any suggestions?

The choices of windows are mind-boggling. As a builder, I have tried a host of products from all different manufacturers, and have come to rely on windows from Andersen, Gilkey, Hurd, Marvin, Pella, Semco and Wheathershield. They are primarily wood window manufacturers, although some have entered the vinyl market. I like wood windows. Besides, if you want to stain the interior, then wood is really your only choice. If you want a frame that is maintenance-free on the outside, these manufacturers offer exterior vinyl or aluminum cladding with endless options of color.

The paint on my house is chipped and peeling. Should I repaint it, or install new siding? If I decide to install new siding, which do you recommend - aluminum or vinyl?

If you want to save money, then painting your house is the way to go. But, as I'm sure you know, you'll be painting it again within the next few years. If you want your house to have that painted look without having to paint, put vinyl siding on your home. Companies such as Alcoa, Wolverine, and CertainTeed all make quality siding that looks great. The vinyl siding is more durable than aluminum. The going rate for vinyl siding, including installation, is between $165.00—$185.00 per square—which is a 10 x 10 foot area.

I want to build a new deck. There are so many different types of decking available, I don't know which to choose. Any suggestions?

The most popular materials available are treated lumber, redwood, cedar, composite and vinyl. Most people prefer to build their decks out of treated lumber because it works well and costs less than the other choices. I really like redwood because it has a great look with minimal warping. But because it is a softer wood, it can more readily chip and scratch. The composite market has been very strong. Composite is made from recycled plastic and wood shavings, so from an environmental perspective, it is a good choice. Because composite saws and shapes just like wood, you won't need any special tools to work with it. Unlike wood, composite won't warp or chip. I recommend a product manufactured by Trex Easy Care Decking. Vinyl is coming on strong as well, and like composite, it won't warp or chip. But, vinyl decking has a much different look than the wood decking. Whatever material you use, you'll have to spend some bucks, so be sure you see samples before you make your choice.

A section of my concrete sidewalk is blistering. Do I just have to live with it, or can I repair it myself?

Blistering is a common problem that occurs when wet cement cures too quickly and outside temperature fluctuates too rapidly. You can fix it, but only temporarily. Go to a home center and buy the smallest bag of Portland cement and a concrete additive mix. The mix looks like a gallon of milk. Clean the sidewalk so it is dust free, and wet it down. Mix the cement with the concrete additive until you get a toothpaste consistency. Apply the mixture using a flat steel trowel (Figure 16). Once it dries, run a soft broom in the same direction as the grain of the walk. You have now repaired your sidewalk, and will probably do it again in a year or two.

Figure 16

What is the best kind of paint to use on my stucco home? I've had some work done on the plaster and I can't find a paint that matches. Please help!

One of the best "paints" for stucco is ThoroCoat®. It's a cement-based coating that is applied over the stucco. The great thing about this coating is that you can tint it to match any color. It is available in five gallon buckets and costs about $90.00. If you are doing a large area, you need to mix the different buckets together so that the color is uniform all the way around your home.

I want to put new roof on my house. There are three layers on it already, can I just put another layer on top of that?

No, in fact it is a law in Illinois and other states. Three is the maximum number of layers allowed on your roof. It's for your own safety as well, unless you want to wear that new roof on your lap. I am not a big re-roofing fan. If you have an old roof that has lasted thirty years, you should tear it off because there are new technologies and ways to make this roof better. This also lets you find out whether the roof is rotting, or has suffered water damage and requires new sheeting. Of course, it cost more money to tear the old roof off, it's easy for me to spend other people's money, but it provides the best results. For more information about state roofing laws, contact the Department of Standards and Regulation.

My asphalt driveway is cracked and damaged in some areas. Can I repair the damage myself, or do I need to re-tar the entire surface?

If your asphalt driveway is in otherwise good condition, repair the cracks yourself, and quickly. The freezing and thawing that occurs due to extreme weather conditions cause those cracks to expand and contract, and will eventually break apart your driveway. There are all kinds of premixed filling compounds available for asphalt in gallon and quart containers, as well as caulk tubes. I recommend products by Bondex® and Sakrete®. They are both high quality and user-friendly. Now you are ready for the fun part! First, grab some water and a steel brush to clean out the cracks and holes. Remove as much dirt and dust as possible and allow to dry overnight. Once dry, fill the cracks according to label directions. It is important to overfill the area slightly because the compound will shrink upon drying (Figure 17). Now, get out your skateboard, you've just added years to your driveway.

Figure 17

TER-3

Plumbing Fix-Its

The pipes in my home make a knocking sound every time I shut off the water faucet in my upstairs bathroom's sink or bathtub. It's driving me crazy! What can I do to stop this noise?

You know if you could get the noise to keep a beat, you could start a band. But there is something you can do. In your plumbing system there are air chambers that act like shock absorbers to cushion the pressure when you turn the water off. Often in older homes, the air escapes from these chambers. You need to drain your pipes in order to replenish the air to your system. First, turn off your main water valve and open all the faucets in your home so the water drains out all of the pipes. Then turn off the faucets, and turn the main valve back on. Finally, remove the screens from all of your faucet spouts and clean any trapped sediment. When you drain the system, sediment loosens and gets caught in the screens. This sediment will reduce your water pressure.

Nowadays, there are so many different types of bathtubs available - from cast iron and steel to plastic and fiberglass. What is the best kind of tub to install if I want the best value for my dollar?

In order of preference, I like cast iron, porcelain composite and fiberglass. I would only use steel as a last resort. The only problem is that a cast iron tub weighs a ton, and it is murder for the plumber and a plumber's helper to get it into the bathroom. But for lasting value and beauty there is no substitute. Many companies manufacture porcelain composite, but the best I have seen is a called Americast® made by American Standard. These composite tubs are durable, and lighter than cast iron. Their finishes seem to last as long as cast iron, though they do chip a little easier. The fiberglass tubs come in many shapes and sizes. Most whirlpool tubs are constructed of fiberglass. So if you are installing a whirlpool, fiberglass is really your only choice. The problem with fiberglass tubs is that they do scratch, and their shine can fade over time. Steel tubs, my last resort, are cheap and nasty and won't last. Enough said.

In the hot weather, my toilet sweats like crazy and the water is ruining my bathroom floor. What can I do?

I'm guessing that you either do not own an air conditioner, or do not use it very much. The tank sweats because the water in the tank is cooler than the air around it. You can buy a kit from your local hardware store to solve this problem. Basically, it is a foam insulation that you put inside your tank. To begin, drain the tank and dry the inside surface. Then, trim the insulation to fit inside your tank and attach it with the adhesive provided. Or, if you're feeling extravagant, you can purchase a non-sweat toilet.

I have a fifteen-year-old, three-gallon toilet that doesn't completely flush. When I flush it, the water in the tank does not empty and the toilet bowl doesn't fill. As a result, whatever is in the toilet won't go down. What can I do?

Your toilet doesn't have enough water pressure due to an obstruction in the throat or the closet flange below the toilet—in other words, between the toilet bowl and the sewer. This is common in older toilets. Get a seven foot-long plumbing snake, it is designed just for toilets. Go right through the toilet bowl and rod it out (Figure 18). Now, the water in the tank will be higher and have enough force and flow to empty into the toilet bowl. You can also try cleaning the holes underneath the rim. Use pipe cleaners and toilet bowl cleaner and clean each hole individually.

Figure 18

Sometimes my hot water heater makes a crackling noise that sounds like it is making popcorn. What is causing this?

Get a little butter, salt, a movie, and you are set. This is a common problem in older hot water heaters. (When you think about it, they're actually cold water heaters.) Calcium and lime can build up at the bottom of the tank. When the burner ignites to heat the water, these deposits heat up and crackle. This condition is typically not a problem, except for making you crave a snack every time you pass the heater, but check a couple things to be certain. First, test the overflow valve which is on the side of the heater and connected to a tube that hangs down almost to the ground (Figure 19). This is a safety valve which you should check every six months. If the water temperature or pressure get too high, this valve will open and release water from the tank. To test it, grab the metal tab at the end of the valve and pull it upwards. Keep in mind, hot water will come out of the pipe, so put a bucket under it. Release the metal tab. If water keeps coming out, then you need to call a plumber to replace the valve. Second, check the water temperature gauge to make sure that the temperature is not too high. The setting that is in the middle is plenty hot for a great bath or shower. If your heater is more than fifteen years old you might consider replacing it. Though a little costly, this is one sure way to eliminate the noise.

open

closed

Figure 19

• overflow valve • drain valve

"Sometimes my two-year-old toilet seems to flush all by itself, though not all the way. What can I do to stop this?"

It sounds like your toilet has a mind of it's own. My guess is that the water level in the toilet is too high. Remove the tank cover and locate the overflow tube—the cylinder that stands in the middle of your tank (Figure 20). If the water level rises higher than the overflow tube, it is too high. (Most overflow tubes have markers indicating proper water level. If the water level rises higher than this marker, it is too high.) Toilets contain either a float ball or a floating-cup ball cock which regulate the water level. If your toilet has a float ball, gently bend the rod that holds the float down towards the bottom of the tank. If your toilet has a floating-cup ball cock, you can reset the tank's water level in one of two ways. Either adjust the screw on top, or adjust the metal clip that holds it in place.

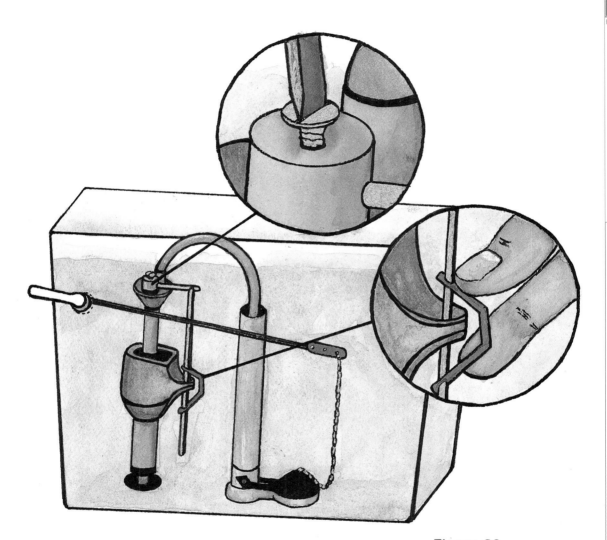

Figure 20

My sump pump seems to run all the time.
I was told that the water table in my area is high.
Is there any risk from this pump running so much?

Your sump pump is just doing its job. With it working so hard, you don't have to worry about the motor going bad, but the switch might go bad. As a maintenance point, this switch should be replaced at least once every three years. You may be able to stop your pump from running constantly. To make sure, unplug the pump and watch the water level in the pit. If the water rises just above the drain pipe inlets and stops, then you can raise the pump off the bottom of the pit floor (See Figure 27 and question 85). Remember that water seeks its own level, it's OK if extra water sits in the pit and the pump runs less.

I am remodeling my home, and as part
of that project I am upgrading my plumbing system.
One plumber recommended cast iron for the drain
and vents, while another suggested plastic pipe.
The cast iron materials cost much more,
are they worth it?

Yes cast iron costs more, but it is hands down the best material for the waste system.
I can't tolerate noisy drain pipes. (I have Niagara Falls in my home from a previous remodeling job.) You can build a nice, quiet system and not break the bank. Speak to your plumber about doing the waste risers in cast iron and the horizontal runs in plastic. Waste risers are the vertical plumbing pipes that connect to the sewer. This way you'll get the best of both worlds—a quiet system at a reasonable price.

The hose bib outside my house freezes every winter. What can I do to stop this?

You need a frost-proof hose bib. It looks very much like a conventional hose bib, except the valve is at the end of a long tube that remains inside your heated home (Figure 24). You should hire a qualified plumber, unless you have a brother-in-law or some relative who has the right tools to install this gizmo. To install a frost-proof hose bib, you must turn off your water and cut the pipes leading to the old valve. Then install the frost-proof unit and connect it to the water line. The type of pipe you have—galvanized iron or copper—will determine how this connection is made. Better yet, let your brother-in-law watch Monday Night Football, and call a plumber.

Figure 21

Water from my upstairs shower is seeping through my kitchen ceiling, but I can't figure out the source of the leak. How can I find it?

This is a tough one. The leak could be originating from the shower drain, the shower base, or the waste piping that lies under the floor or in the ceiling. The best way to detect its source, although you won't want to do this, is to open the ceiling. Then with the shower running, you can find the leak. If you don't want to tear apart your ceiling just yet, you can try the poke and hope method. Remove the screen from the shower drain and install a test plug. You can get a test plug at a plumbing supply shop. Let the water fill just below the top of the shower pan. Then, go downstairs and wait (and hope) for the water to trickle down. If it does, the problem is in the seat of the shower drain or at the shower base, and requires just a quick caulking job. To do so, dry the area thoroughly and apply some silicone caulk around the joint (Figure 22). Let dry for 24 hours. If this method doesn't work, then you should open up your ceiling. A leak that originates in the piping could require a qualified plumber.

Figure 22

My sewer needs to be rodded about every two years. Do I need a new sewer pipe? If so, there are a lot of trees growing near the sewer, how could I prevent a new pipe from getting clogged with roots?

Depending on where you live, you could replace your cast iron or clay pipes with plastic pipes. Check with you local Building Department to find out. These roots can eventually break through the cast iron and clay pipes, but they cannot get through the plastic. I know it sounds backwards, but it is true. I suggest that you televise your sewer using a sewer camera—that is right, a camera that goes in your sewer and sends an image back to a video screen. It is better than a documentary about raising the Titanic. Then you can see exactly what is inside the sewer pipe, and decide what to do. You can either hire a contractor to do this for around $400—$500, or rent one yourself for about $100 a day. Have fun.

I want to remodel my bathroom to include a whirlpool tub. How much space do I need to install one? Which models do you recommend?

There are whirlpool tubs that are the same size as a standard tub. But if you're like me, when you go to soak in a whirlpool you want to stretch out and relax, not be scrunched up like a pretzel. If you are limited by space, a standard-sized tub sells for about $650. A two-person tub sells for about $1,000. It is 42" wide x 72" long, and that is exactly how much space you need to install one. Each tub requires some electrical work. I really like the whirlpool tubs by Jaccuzi®, but Kohler Co., American Standard, and a few others also make good, solid products in all kinds of shapes and sizes.

My shower faucet is leaking.
My friend told me to change the cartridge.
Is this true? How do I change it?

I would hire a plumber, then all you have to do is write the check. But if you want to do this yourself, it is a relatively easy task. For this explanation, I'll assume that you have a single-lever shower faucet. First, turn off the main water valve to your home. With a single-level shower faucet, there is a plastic cap in the center of the handle. Use a screw driver to flip off the cap. Underneath, you'll find a small screw. Remove this screw and the handle should come off. There you will find a shaft that is held in place by a retaining clip or by another screw. Remove this and grasp the shaft with a pair of pliers to pull the cartridge right out (See Figure 23 and question 60). If it is stuck, add some vinegar to an empty spray bottle and apply it to the shaft. The vinegar will loosen the scale and salt that may be holding the bugger in place. Then, march down to your local plumbing supply house and ask for a new cartridge. Just remember, when replacing the cartridge it has to line up just right. There is a slot to insure proper alignment, this is not something you want to beat in with a hammer.

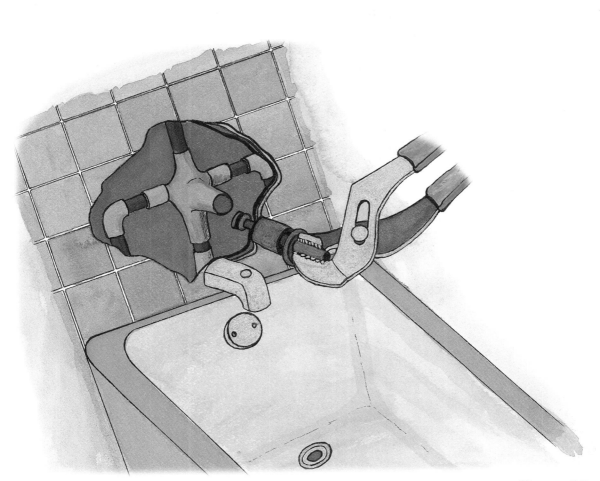

Figure 23

My water pressure is getting weaker and weaker. When I use the shower, it feels like a fine rain. What can I do to increase the pressure?

I could write an entire book on weak water pressure. In your case, it sounds like there is calcium buildup in the shower valve. To be certain, test the shower without the valve. Get someone to help you, so one of you can be in the bathroom, while the other turns off the water main. Now turn off the water main, and remove the valve assembly in the shower faucet (See Figure 23 and question 59). Turn on the water main back on. If the water shoots out of the wall like a water park, then you know the problem is in the valve. Simply clean the cartridge valve assembly by soaking it in vinegar and using an old toothbrush to scrub it out. Now replace the valve. Get ready for a nice, strong shower.

see illustration on previous page

The drain in my basement is emitting a sewer odor. I've poured bleach down there but the smell returns a few days later. What can I do to eliminate this?

First, make sure that when you look down into the drain you see standing water. If the water is there, you know that the trap is still in place. If there is no water, you need to open the floor and replace the trap. Big job, get help. If the trap is in place, the odor is caused by bacteria in your sewer system. Pour about a quart of hydrogen peroxide down the drain and let it stand overnight. The next day, flush water through the drain and repeat the operation. The hydrogen peroxide kills any bacteria that may be growing in your system. Believe it or not, it really works.

Sometimes when I flush my toilet on the second floor, the water level in the downstairs toilet goes up and down, and on occasion, it partially flushes. What causes this and how can I stop it?

It sounds like you have a venting problem in your home's waste and vent system. Most likely the plumbing stack—the thing that sticks out from the roof —has some type of blockage. You can inspect it and rod it out yourself provided you have the right tools. I recommend calling a licensed and bonded plumber.

I want a no muss-no fuss kitchen faucet.
Which kind should I buy?

There are scores of excellent faucets on the market from companies such as Moen Inc.,

Kohler Co. and Grohe, to name a few. Just remember, you get what you pay for. Don't

try to cut corners and buy some cheap faucet because it costs less than the name brands.

I recommend that you purchase it from a plumbing supply house, where you can get a

great deal on a quality product.

The toilet in my bathroom is too close to the vanity cabinet. Can I move the toilet over a little, or do I need to buy a new cabinet? My husband says this is a big job and that I should just leave it alone.

Well, you could purchase a new vanity, but it would have to be smaller than the original one. Plus, you will need to disconnect the sink and then reinstall the whole thing. Listen to your husband and forget it! You could install an offset flange. The flange holds the toilet in place with those two bolts you see on either side of the toilet bowl's base (Figure 24). An offset flange allows you to move the toilet over about two inches. You will probably need a plumber to complete this job, but you would have needed one anyway for the vanity fiasco. And, installing an offset flange is much cheaper in labor and materials.

Figure 24

CHAP

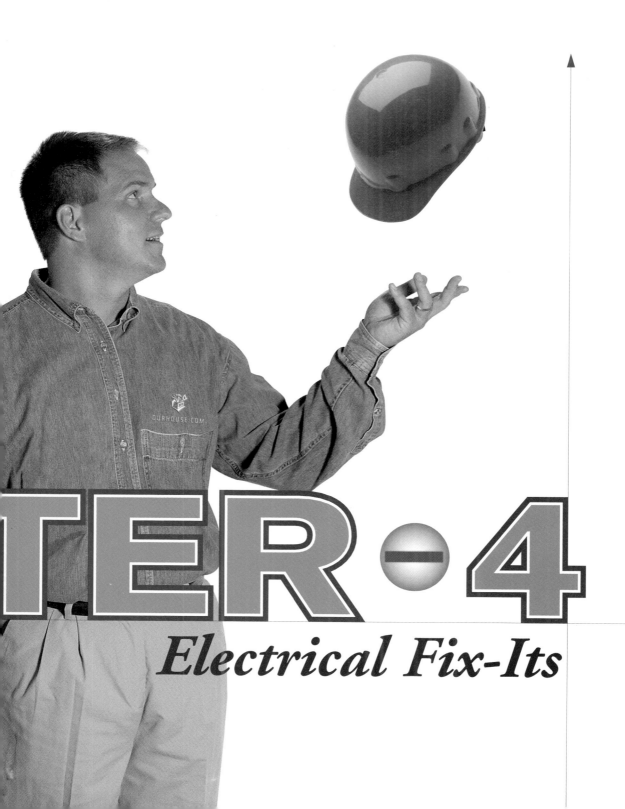

TER-4

Electrical Fix-Its

I have recessed lights in my family room. After they've been on for a while, some turn off all by themselves, then turn on again later. Is there something wrong with the fixture or the wiring?

It sounds like you have too much wattage in your cottage. These lights are actually doing their job. The recessed lights contain a thermal protection device that shuts the light off when it gets too hot. In other words, a bulb that is too bright generates too much heat. Turn the lights off and remove one bulb. Inside the fixture are instructions that list the maximum wattage or wattage rating. Do not exceed the recommended wattage rating. This presents a potential fire hazard. If this does not solve your problem, contact a qualified electrician to inspect the fixture and ensure that it was installed correctly.

There is an outlet in my living room controlled by a single switch. This switch is on one side of the room, and I want to add another switch on the other side of the room. How can I do it?

Boy that is easy. Not! What your asking about is a three-way switch. If your home is set up with electrical conduit, you can hire (I said HIRE) an electrician to add the switch to the other side of the room. Or if you have a switch at the other end of the room that controls something else, the electrician will just have to run some additional wires, and then change the type of switch. However if there is no switch at the other end, the electrician must cut in a new switch box and run some new pipes and wires through the wall to accommodate your request. For each of these three scenarios, I strongly recommend that you hire an electrician to do the job.

I want to upgrade the electrical service to my home. Right now I have a 60-amp service. Should I upgrade to a 100 or 200-amp service? How must does this cost?

The amount of service you need for your home is directly proportional to the amount of power you use. (Don't I sound like I know what I'm talking about?) For example, if you have a dishwasher, air conditioner, computer, microwave, electric dryer, garbage disposal and stuff like that (read that again using the voice of Roseanne Rosanna-Dana), a 100-amp service is plenty to run your home. But, a 200-amp service allows room for expansion. Considering resale value, I recommend a 200-amp service. Since you have to pay for an upgrade anyway, the cost increase from a 100-amp to a 200-amp service is minimal. To upgrade to a 200-amp service, you can expect to pay anywhere from $1,200-1,900.

I am building a new home. What do I need to know about its electrical system?

As an extension of question 67, take a good look at what you are going to have in your new home. Thirty years ago homes had limited electrical capability, one or two fuses or circuit breakers controlled entire floors. Today, housing codes require countless dedicated circuits, and for good reason. For example, in a new home one circuit breaker in the electrical panel controls just the refrigerator, and another controls just the dishwasher. So if you intend to run a dishwasher, an air conditioner, a computer, a microwave, an electric dryer, etc., your electrical system must be sized accordingly. The most important thing you can do is hire a qualified and knowledgeable electrical contractor to install your electrical system. This electrical contractor can do a load calculation, which is required in most cities and villages. Take time to meet your contractor as well as the other contractors building your new home. Chances are if you bring doughnuts a couple of times you may get a few freebies in addition to an expert job. Hey, it has always worked for me, and over the years I have learned that success on the construction site can be determined by a good Boston cream.

I want to install a ceiling fan in my kitchen to replace a ceiling light fixture. Can I just buy any fan and install it into the same box?

Well, yes and no. Remove the old light fixture and inspect the box in the ceiling. If the box is attached to a ceiling joist (a piece of wood) go ahead and install your new fan. If your home was built within the last twenty years, chances are the contractor set the box up to accept a ceiling fan. If the box is loose and you can wiggle it, you'll need to modify the way it is mounted (Figure 25). I strongly recommend that you hire an electrician to do this job. Your electrical system is one area of your home where you don't want to take any chances. Once you are certain that the box is secure, you can install the fan of your choice.

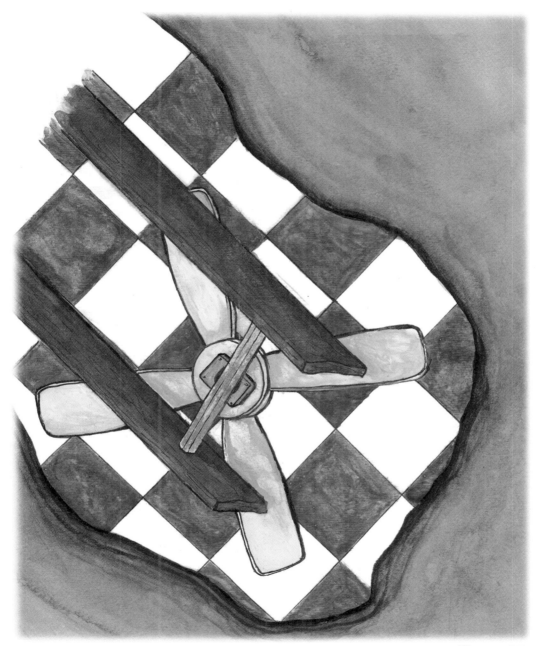

Figure 25

I have a computer and some hi-tech stereo equipment in my home. Should I be using surge protectors? Which type do you recommend?

Yes, yes, yes! Of course you should be using a surge protector. And here is a curious paradox. You have all of this really expensive equipment, say thousands of dollars' worth, and you want to protect it with a $10 surge protector. NOT! As with most things in life, you get what you pay for. A really good surge protector starts at $50. Next time you visit the computer or electronics store, ask your salesperson for the best surge protector in the store, and buy it.

The electrical system in my city home is pipe and wire, you know, conduit. My sister lives in a different county and her house is wired using a product called Romex®. Is it better than the conduit? Can I install Romex® in my home, or am I restricted by where I live?

I am not a big fan of running extension cord through my walls to power my house. To me Romex® is just that. I know I will get in trouble for saying this, but most people in this country use Romex®. Well, just because Billy jumped off a bridge doesn't mean that I have to jump. Conduit is really the safest way to wire your house, and offers you more choices down the line. For example, say you want to install a ceiling fan, and you want the fan and the light to have a separate switch by the door. If your home has conduit wiring and that ceiling box is already there, you just need an additional wire, a new switch, and poof you are ready to install your fan. With Romex®, you need to open the ceiling and the wall to accomplish the same thing. I would always prefer conduit in my home.

How do I determine if a circuit is overloaded? How many outlets can a single circuit support?

I am always leery about giving advice concerning your home's electrical system. I don't want to scare you, but mistakes can cost you your life. So if you're not 100% certain, hire a qualified electrician. OK, I'm off my soap box. Everything in your electrical system is sized by load. The amount of dedicated circuits you need is proportional to the amount of power you use. For example, the receptacles (outlets) in your living room that control the lights, the vacuum cleaner, and the answering machine do not carry a heavy load. In this case, one circuit can support six to ten receptacles. A sure sign that the circuit breaker is overloaded is if it trips, or interrupts the flow of power. This is what the breaker does to prevent a fire when there is too much electricity flowing through the circuit. So don't mess around, get an electrician to check it out. It is money well spent.

I am remodeling my kitchen, and I was told that I must add new circuits to bring my house up to code. Is this true?

The new National Electrical Code® (NEC) and your local electrical code are very specific. You might be amazed by the number of circuits that are required for your kitchen alone. Each of the following appliances must have their own dedicated circuit: refrigerator, dishwasher, garbage disposal, microwave oven, conventional oven, as well as counter receptacles and light fixtures. Any other appliance you have for your culinary desires also requires its own dedicated circuit. So in answer to your question—yes, you need to update these circuits to keep you and your family safe.

I am adding central air conditioning to
my home and my electrical box is full.
Do I need to update my electrical service?

Yes. Next question.

What are some questions I should ask before hiring an electrician?

How do they take their coffee? Do they prefer Boston cream donuts or powdered sugar donuts? First, find out if they are licensed, most municipalities require electrician's to be licensed. Then, inquire about their work. Do they have experience with the type of project that you want completed? Of course, as with any contractor, you need references. Take the time to call these references and ask about on-the-job performance. See the Chapter Six entitled, "Choosing a Contractor," for complete overview.

When my refrigerator kicks on, the lights in the family room go dim. Is this something I should worry about?

Yes. Your refrigerator is probably not on its own circuit, and it is overloading the circuit breaker. This is not a good thing. If it does have its own circuit, it could be sharing the neutral wire—the white one—with another device. Either way, this is a problem that must be corrected.

I am constantly changing the light bulbs on my outdoor light fixtures. Can you recommend a good brand of light bulb that will last a long time?

It is really not the brand, but the type of bulb you choose. Light bulbs with higher wattage dissipate more heat. In a concealed fixture—one that covers the bulb from the elements—this high heat shortens the light bulb's life. So choose the lowest possible wattage for your fixtures that gives you the desired light. But that's not all folks. Buy light bulbs that are 130 volts (V). The average bulbs you buy at the grocery store are 120 V, and these burn out faster. The 130 V bulbs have a thicker filament and last an average of 40% longer. You can also try the new fluorescent bulbs that can last up to two years.

My daughter told me that I need to install ground fault circuit interrupters (GFCIs) in the electrical outlets in my kitchen and bathrooms. My house is about forty years old, and she said that without them it is unsafe. Is this true?

Don't you just hate when your kids start telling you what to do? Especially when they are right. Find solace in that fact that the reason she is so smart is because she is your daughter. Yes, you should install them. The GFCI receptacles are those funny-looking outlets you see in newer homes around the kitchen sink and in bathrooms (Figure 26). Basically, they are mini-electrical panels that detect an electrical short or a power surge in less than a half of a second, and stop the current flowing through the unit. The National Electrical Code® (NEC) requires that GFCI receptacles must be in place where there is an outlet within touching distance from water. That is, if you are washing your dishes at your kitchen sink and can reach over and plug in your toaster, you need to install a GFCI. Available at any hardware store or home center, GFCIs cost about ten dollars and come complete with installation instructions. This is an easy thing you can do yourself, and it is great way to get your daughter off of your back. Remember, if you are not completely comfortable doing electrical work, hire someone to do it. Or better yet, get that smarty pants daughter of yours to do it for you!

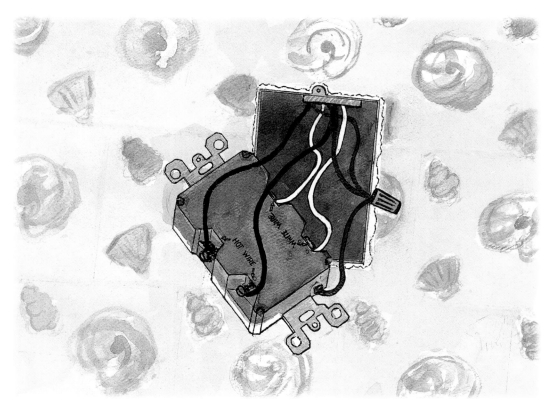

Figure 26

The wiring in my home is about 70-years-old. Should I hire an electrician to rewire my home? How much does it cost?

If this is something you have been worrying about, then I'd say yes. Seventy years ago before the modern age of plastic, homes were equipped with cloth-coated wires. As this wiring ages, it breaks down and has the potential to short circuit. Will this happen? Probably not, but it could. To rewire a typical 2,000 square-foot home should cost approximately $4,000—$6,000. It is not cheap, but it is a good selling point down the line.

I have two phone lines in my home.
When my wife is talking on one line,
she can hear me talking on my business line.
How can I eliminate this problem?

Solving phone problems is the biggest pain in the neck, who allowed this one in the book?

You could be hearing each other for one of three reasons. First, the phone line is improperly

grounded (I bet that is it). Second, the connection on the two lines is crossed somewhere

(good luck trying to find it). Third, the quality of the phone wire is not very good. Try

using a stranded wire for your phone system. And yes I would hire an electrician, and let a

professional sweat it out.

My husband installed a Casablanca® fan in our kitchen, and now, every so often the fan turns on all by itself. What is happening? Do we need an electrician?

Do you have an Intellatouch® switch? I bet you do. This switch is a great invention that Casablanca® devised. It lets you install a multi-function switch in an opening that has only a two-wire connection. With this switch you can turn on the light, the fan, and control the fan speed from one location. It is a transmitter (like a radio) that sends a signal to your fan and tells it what to do. The mysterious start-up is caused by radio frequencies from other electronic devices in your area, such as a cellular phone, a cordless phone, even an airplane. Call Casablanca® and see if they can send you a different switch to control your fan that uses a different radio band width.

How often should I test my surge protectors and smoke detectors?

Test your surge protectors, smoke detectors and carbon monoxide detectors every month.

Check their batteries every six months. I check my batteries when I change the clocks.

Can I replace a 15-amp circuit-breaker with a 20-amp breaker?

No, the size of your electrical system is determined by the load it carries (remember?), or in other words, the amount of power you use. The size of your circuit breaker is the most important component of that relationship. Boosting the breaker size is asking for trouble.

Can I replace the circuit-breaker in my electrical panel with a breaker from a different manufacturer?

Well if you talk to any circuit breaker manufacturer, they would say no. And I agree. The interchangeable brands are quite expensive and the quality is usually lousy. Whether you have a circuit breaker made by Square D or General Electric, I would stay with the same brand. It just makes a more consistent and better looking job.

CHAP

TER · 5

Mechanical System Maintenance

My four-year-old home has a sump pump and an ejector pump. What type of maintenance do these pumps require?

Great question! Most homeowners never think about the mechanical aspects of their homes, when it is really one of the most important elements of good housekeeping. Underneath each pump is a pit (See Figure 27 and question 53). Now you may not like this, but each pit must be cleaned every year. YUCK. This prevents obstructions from entering the system and impeding your pump's performance. Also, within these pits is a submersible switch that must be changed every three years. So bring a shovel and a bullet to bite, you're doing a good thing.

Figure 27

I have hot water heat in my home, and I would like to install central air-conditioning. What system do you recommend? How much will it cost?

You have two options. First, you can install a Space Pack which is a central cooling system that provides cool air via flexible duct work. This means that your contractor must cut and poke holes in your walls and ceilings to thread the ducts throughout your home. Once completed, these holes must be patched and painted (yada, yada, yada). Now this is a lot of work, but the system really works well if the contractor knows how to do it right. Your second option is a ductless air-conditioning system, yes folks you heard it here, this is the wave of the future for people with hot water heat. I'm sure you have stayed at a hotel before and noticed the unit by the window that controls the room's heating and cooling. That is the concept here, but what you see inside resembles an over-sized duct with the thermostat mounted on the wall like a regular system (Figure 28). The only mess is caused by the condensation line that runs to the compressor outside. (You know that big fan thing.) You will need more than one unit to cool an entire house, but the cost savings compared to duct work system will be substantial. Ask your heating and cooling specialist about this one, it is going to be big.

Figure 28

What is the best kind of furnace filter to use?
What is your opinion of electrostatic
filters? Are they worth the expense?

Yes, they do work. There is one that you can have installed in your system that only needs to be replaced once a year, called Space Gard®. It does a great job of controlling dust and gunk in your home. This filter costs about $350 to install, plus about $30 each year to replace it. A less expensive alternative to the electrostatic filter is a pleated filter. The 3M Corp. manufactures these filters at a cost of $10-15. A company called American Air Filter (AAF International) makes a pleated filter comparable to 3M's at half the cost. That is the one I use and it works great. It is recommended that you replace them every three months, but I change mine every month. Whatever you do, stop buying those nasty, worthless filters that only cost a dollar! You might as well send me the money, because I can filter the air in your home better from my house than those things.

Five minutes after the heat from my forced-air furnace goes on and off, the furnace makes loud banging noise. What is this, and how can I get rid of it?

I have been hearing this from a lot of people. What happens is after the furnace heats your home, the duct work gets good and warm and the metal expands (recall your high school physics). As the system cools down, the expanded metal shrinks and can sometimes make noise. Set yourself down with a chair and a newspaper next to the furnace and beneath the main duct work. As the furnace cools, listen and locate the bang. Once you find it's source, wedge a broomstick or a 2x4 from the floor and push it up almost bending the duct. Repeat the heating and cooling process. If the noise is gone, slightly bend that area to keep the metal from popping again. If you get good at this, you could make extra money on the weekends while you read the newspaper!

How often should my furnace be cleaned and serviced? Is this something I can do myself?

No you should not do this yourself. For piece of mind, I recommend that you have it cleaned and serviced every year. The last thing you need is to have your furnace clunk out in the middle of February and leave you with frost on your toes. The best time to have this done is in the spring. At that point an HVAC technician can also service your air conditioner. The cost for this maintenance is about $50-75.

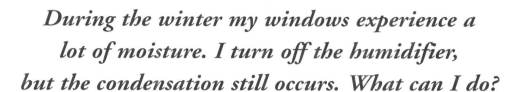

*During the winter my windows experience a
lot of moisture. I turn off the humidifier,
but the condensation still occurs. What can I do?*

Do you take showers in the winter, or cook, or breathe? All of these things add moisture to the air in your home. The average family of four expels four gallons of water or moisture per day. It is important, especially in the winter, to exhaust this moisture as much as possible. Run your exhaust fans after you take a shower, and let them run for at least half an hour. When you are cooking, use your fan as well. Run your ceiling fans on low, it will not only cut down on the moisture, but it will keep your home at a more even temperature. In fact, most of the excess moisture occurs because we do not utilize the fans we have in our homes. I would tell you to limit your breathing, but that may be a bit much.

Do I need to perform routine maintenance on my hot water heater?

Yes, I recommend that you test the overflow valve (also known as pressure valve) every six months, and drain the tank every year. The overflow valve sticks out of the side of the heater up at the top, with a pipe that runs down the side and goes to nowhere (Figure 29). To test it, grab the metal tab at the end of the valve and pull it upwards. Keep in mind, hot water will come out of the pipe, so put a bucket under it. Release the metal tab. To drain the tank, first turn off the water valve at the top of the tank and turn off the burner. Now, open the valve at the bottom of the tank (See Figure 19 and question 51). You can attach a hose to the valve so the water will empty right into your basement drain. Again, remember the water is HOT. When completed, turn the water valve and the burner back on. And it is not a hot water heater, it is a cold water heater. Think about that one, Grasshopper.

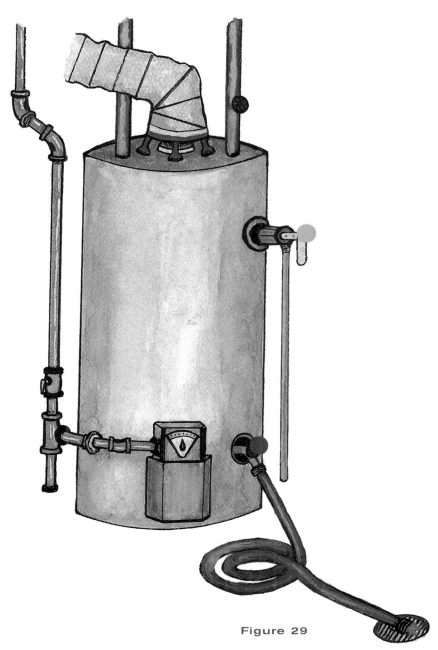

Figure 29

• overflow valve   • drain valve

I am adding a room onto my home. How can I determine if my existing furnace can handle the added space? Is there some formula to follow?

Hire a heating, ventilation and air conditioning (HVAC) contractor to inspect and even clean the unit, because there are many factors that determine heater capacity. A contractor can accurately calculate the number of heat runs, the number of returns, the room size, the number of windows, and the heat loss and gain. Remember, bigger is not always better. A furnace that is too big will constantly turn on and off, which will shorten the life of the unit and cause uneven temperatures in your home.

The heat in my home is really spotty, such that some rooms are too cool while others are too hot. How can I adjust my furnace to balance the temperature throughout my house?

Your answer is in your question, you need to balance your system. You can do this by opening and closing the registers. If a room is too hot, close the register 90% of the way. This will increase the pressure to the rooms that are too cold. It will take a few days of trial and error, but it works. Another trick is to switch your fan motor to "Fan On" instead of "Auto." This will constantly circulate the air and provide a more even temperature. Don't worry about the fan motor burning out, a motor wears out faster if it is turned on and off all the time.

See illustration on next page

I want to install a programmable thermostat, but I've noticed that they are expensive. Are they worth the cost? Can you recommend a reliable model?

They are costly, but well worth it. Especially if you are not home during the day. You can program the thermostat to turn down the temperature after you go to work, and kick it up right before you get home; then, turn down the temperature while you are sleeping. It's not unheard of to save 30% on your energy costs in one year. So when you calculate this savings toward the $100 you spend on a programmable thermostat, it is well worth it. I recommend a model manufactured by White-Rodgers.

Figure 30

What is the best humidifier unit for a house?

Insist on Aprilaire®, it is the industry standard.

Which furnace is better, an 80-plus or 90-plus efficiency unit? What advice can you give me before I hire an HVAC contractor to install a new furnace in my home?

They are both great choices. It really comes down to how much you want to spend, and how long you intend to live in your home. A 90-plus furnace costs about $800 more than the 80-plus unit. So the first thing you should calculate is how long it will take to recover the furnace's cost against your energy savings. If you install an 80-plus unit, you will need to invest in a chimney liner. Your old pig furnace loses heat that gets pushed up and out of the chimney with the other spent gases. With the energy efficient 80-plus model, there is not enough heat being forced into your chimney to draft out the spent gases. These trapped gases create condensation, and may also cause carbon monoxide backup. A chimney liner helps to regulate these gases, and is required in most cities and villages. A new liner costs about $400, including installation. The 90-plus furnace can be directly vented to the outside wall of your home. Meaning there is no chimney (or liner) required. As far as choosing a heating, ventilation and air conditioning (HVAC) contractor, make sure that they have a license, have experience in the trade, and can provide references (see Chapter Six entitled, "Choosing a Contractor"). When it comes to your home's mechanical systems, service is very important. So make sure the contractor you choose has a proven record of service.

My home is built on a slab with the heating ducts set in the slab. I've noticed that the ducts accumulate water after a heavy rain. What is causing this? How can I fix it, Mr. Fix-It?

Hey, I am supposed to be the funny guy, Funny Guy. Sadly, you have problems. It sounds like the duct work has disintegrated. And, the water table near you must be high. You could try sinking a sump pump pit somewhere in your home, in a mechanical room if you have one. So when the water level rises, the pit will collect the water and the pump will get rid of it. The only other options are to either break up the concrete and install new duct work (which is crazy), or run new duct work in the ceiling and abandon the ducting in the floor.

My furnace starts up and shuts down to heat my home as it should. Then, a few minutes later, it kicks on for about two more minutes and shuts down again. What is happening?

I bet the limit switch on your unit is bad. A limit switch detects the temperature of the heat exchanger which tells the blower motor when to shut off. If this switch is bad, this motor can run willy nilly like yours. Hire a qualified heating, ventilation and air conditioning (HVAC) contractor to look at it.

I am adding central air-conditioning to my forced air heating system. I want to put the outside fan unit under my deck, but my neighbor says that this is a bad idea. Is this true?

The condensing unit you are referring to should not, repeat should not go under a deck. These units need a lot of air to function properly. Placed under a deck, the hot air it is dispensing gets trapped which dramatically decreases its efficiency. I know you don't want to see it, but you probably don't want a Christmas card from the electric company either.

MECHANICAL SYSTEM MAINTAINENCE

My home has central air-conditioning. When the system operates during the summer cooling months, I notice some hot and cold spots in my home. What can I do?

It sounds like you need to balance the system just like question 93. To do this, open and close the registers in each room. If one room is too cold, close the register to limit the amount of flow to that space. By doing this, you increase the flow of cool air to the other rooms in your home. Next, switch your thermostat from "Auto" to "Fan On" to keep the temperature uniform and reduce the workload on your condensing unit (that big fan thing) outside. This saves electricity and money.

My sump pump hole is very dry.
For the past two weeks is has been emanating an
odor. What is causing it? How can I get rid of it?

You need to raise the water level so that the sump pump is always sitting in water.

Without water, your drain tile is exposed, and is the most likely culprit of the smell. Get a

couple of bricks and put them beneath the sump pump. Then add enough water to the pit

to cover the input pipes. As an extra measure, you can sanitize your pump pit before you

add the water. Pour a couple of quarts of straight hydrogen peroxide in a bucket and use a

brush to scrub the pit. This will kill any odor causing bacteria.

5
CHAPTER

MECHANICAL SYSTEM MAINTAINENCE

CHAP

TER·6
Choosing a Contractor

Choosing a Contractor

So you want to know how to choose a contractor? The business of home building and remodeling has a rather bad reputation. In recent surveys the only group with a lower opinion rating is lawyers (which I can understand). Sometimes it seems that anyone who owns a pickup truck can claim to be a contractor. We all know that this is just not true. Every industry has it's shysters, but you needn't get too discouraged. I have been a builder for more than fourteen years in the Chicagoland area. I consider myself (and since it's my book I get to say this) as good as any person to work with when it comes to building or renovating a home. And, there are hosts of happy homeowners to prove it! I have worked with many contractors and, just like you, I have been extremely happy at times and extremely disappointed at others. There are a handful of good contractors out there no matter where you live, but the trick is finding them.

First, most good contractors do little or no advertising, because word of mouth is a more powerful tool. So ask around, and ask a few people their opinion of a potential contractor. The problem is that the good contractors are very busy, so you may have to do a little leg work yourself to help move along the project. Most important, make sure that this contractor is proficient in your required area of remodeling, I mean you wouldn't hire a plumber to rewire you house! Request to see other jobs like yours. Take the time to go see the projects, and to speak with the former clients. The highest compliment for a contractor is if a past client can say they would work with that person again. Secondly, make sure that you personally like the contractor, and can imagine this person spending weeks, sometimes months working in your home every day. You will spend a lot of time talking to and listening to this person. They will become a part of your family, especially if you are doing a large project. I can recall, on many occasions, taking the clients' children to school because they were running late for work.

Finally, find out if the contractor is a member if any professional organizations, such as the Home Builders Association, or the National Association of the Remodeling Industry. Being a member of such associations requires an investment of time and money. This shows that the contractor is serious about remodeling and intends to be in this industry for the long haul.

If you can find a contractor that meets these criteria, hire that person and get to work!

Lou Manfredini

1. Interiors and Exteriors

Interior/Exterior Caulk:
DAP ALEX PLUS Acrylic Latex Plus
Silicone
DAP Inc.
2400 Boston St.
Suite 200
Baltimore, MD 21224
(800) 543-3840
www.dap.com
Just about every painter uses this product.
It is also good for exteriors, if you cannot
find the one from N.P.C. Sealants.

N.P.C. Solar Seal®
N.P.C. Sealants
P.O. Box 645
Maywood, IL 60153
(708) 681-1040
This is the best exterior caulk. Used exclu-
sively by contractors, until now. Find it,
buy it, use it, and be happy!

Interior Exterior Paints/Primers:
Benjamin Moore & Co.
51 Chestnut Ridge Rd.
Montvale, NJ 07645
(888) 236-6667
www.benjaminmoore.com
For your money, I've found this
paint provides the most consistent
and longlasting finish.

B-I-N® Primer Sealer
Bulls Eye® 1-2-3 Primer Sealer
William Zinsser & Co., Inc.
Somerset, NJ 08875
(732) 469-8100
www.zinsser.com
Wow, what a primer! You can use it
inside and out. Plus, it's water based
for easy clean-up.

Wood Restoration Systems:
Liquid Wood
WoodEpox
Abatron Inc.
5501 95th Ave.
Kenosha, WI 53144
(414) 653-2000
www.abatron.com
If you have rotten wood and want to repair
it, this is the stuff. I've never used a product
that worked as well fixing damaged wood.

2. Exteriors

Decking Materials:
Trex Easy Care Decking
220 S. Cameron St.
Winchester, VI 22601
(800) 289-8739
www.trex.com
One of the first synthetic decking materials
on the market, it shapes, cuts and looks like
wood, but it is virtually maintenance-free.

Exterior Stains/Wood Preservatives:
Cabot® Stains
Samuel Cabot Inc.
100 Hale St.
Newberryport, MA 01950
(800) 877-8246
www.cabotstain.com
This is the best line of exterior wall and
deck stains on the market. Even *Consumer
Reports* rated it the best.

Wolman® Wood Care Products
3020 William Pitt Way
Pittsburgh, PA 15238
(800) 556-7737
www.wolman.com
These are fabulous products for
decks and siding.

Roofing Materials:
GAF Materials Corp.
1361 Alps Rd.
Wayne, NJ 07470
(800) roof411
www.gaf.com
This is a fantastic fiberglass-based shingle that looks like cedar shakes without all the problems.

Globe Building Materials
2230 Indianapolis Blvd.
Whiting, IN 46394
(219) 473-4500
www.globebuildingmtls.com
They make a wonderful asphalt-based shingle that is heavy weight and long lasting.

Vinyl Siding:
CertainTeed Corp.
P.O. Box 860
750 E. Swedesford Rd.
Valley Forge, PA 19482
(800) 233-8990
www.certainteed.com
This is a great line of siding. They also make windows, insulation, roofing, and ventilation products.

Wolverine Siding Systems
P.O. Box 860
750 E. Swedesford Rd.
Valley Forge, PA 19482
(800) 782-8777
www.vinylsiding.com
They make just about the best stuff on the market. It isn't cheap, but it looks awesome and is available in a wide variety of styles.

Vinyl Windows:
Gilkey Window Co.
Cincinnati, OH 45241
(800) 878-7771
www.gilkey.com
A lot of these windows are alike, but these are some of the best I've seen. They install them as well-no middle people.

Wood Windows:
Hurd Millwork Co.
575 Whelen Ave.
Medford, WI 54451
(715) 748-2011
www.hurd.com
A veteran manufacturer of wood windows, their entry into the vinyl market has been strong. Probably because they are good windows, and are available in just about every style at a good price.

Marvin Windows & Doors
P.O. Box 100
Warroad, MN 56763
(800) 441-0007
www.marvin.com
They make quality windows. Everyone thinks they only make custom sizes, but Marvin is competitively priced for standard size windows as well.

Pella Corp.
102 Mainstreet
Pella, IA 50219
(800) 54-pella
www.pella.com
Another fine window manufacturer. They offer some specialty features such as roll screens and shades between the panes of glass.

3. Interiors

Counter tops:
Corian® (by DuPont)
Parksite Inc.
1563 Hubbard Ave.
Batavia, IL 60510
(800) 338-3355
www.corian.com
I am a huge Corian® fan. Mrs. Fix-It and I
have it our home and we love it! If you are
someone who enjoys cooking and entertaining, this is the surface for your kitchen.

Exhaust Fans:
Broan Manufacturing Co.
9236 W. State St.
Hartford, WI 53027
(800) 692-7626
www.broan.com
These are wonderful and quiet fans for
your whole house. I use them a lot.

Paints/Primers:
Perma-White Mildew-Proof Bathroom Paint
Mildew Proof Bathroom Paint
William Zinsser & Co., Inc.
Somerset, NJ 08875
(908) 469-8100
www.zinsser.com
This is a great product for painting a
bathroom or any room where there is
a lot of moisture.

Patching Plaster/Spackling:
Bondex International, Inc.
3616 Scarlet Oak Blvd.
Kirkwood, MO 63122
(800) 231-6781
Bondex makes a complete line of patching
products for walls, floors, and driveways.
They work great.

Wallpaper Strippers:
DIF® Wallpaper Stripper
William Zinsser & Co., Inc.
Somerset, NJ 08875
(908) 469-8100
www.zinsser.com
They make two kinds, one is a gel that
seems to be less messy. They also make tools
to do the job faster.

4. Plumbing

Plumbing Fixtures:
American Standard
P.O. Box 90318
Richmond, VA 23230
(800) 524-9797
www.americanstandard.com
Another fine manufacturer with a lot of
unique styles. They make my favorite
kitchen sink —the Silhouette®.

Elkay Plumbing Products
2222 Camden Ct.
Oak Brook, IL 60523
(630) 574-8484
www.elkay.com
If you're looking for a stainless steel sink,
buy it from Elkay.

Kohler Plumbing Products, Co.
444 Highland Dr.
Kohler, WI 53044
(800) 4-Kohler
www.kohlerco.com
I use their products almost exclusively for
toilets, sinks, and bath tubs. They also make
some nice valves.

Moen Inc.
25300 Al Moen Drive
North Olmstead, OH 44070
(800) 289-6636
www.moen.com
For the money, I think they make the best
worry-free valves on the market. These
valves just keep working and working.

5. Mechanical Systems
Cold Water Heaters:
Reem Manufacturing Co.
P.O. Box 244020
Montgomery, AL 36124
(800) 432-8373
Ask any plumber, Reem is the choice when
installing a new cold water heater.

Furnaces:
Reem Manufacturing Co.
P.O. Box 244020
Montgomery, AL 36124
(800) 432-8373
Another fine line of products from
a fine company.

Weil-McLain - A United Dominion Co.
500 Blaine St.
Michigan City, IN 46360
(219) 879-6561
www.weil-mclain.com
One of the finest names in the business,
with a great warranty to boot.

Furnace Filters:
AAF International
215 Central Ave.
Louisville, KY 40208
(800) 927-6789
www.aafintl.com

This is a filter that slips into (where else?)
the furnace filter slot. 3M also makes them
for about $12-$15 per filter, while
American's cost about $6. Which would
you choose?

Space Gard®
Research Products Corp.
P.O. Box 1467
Madison, WI 53701
(608) 257-8801
www.resprod.com
This is a filter for your forced air system
that lasts for an entire year, really!

Humidifiers:
Aprilaire®
Research Products Corp.
P.O. Box 1467
Madison, WI 53701
(608) 257-8801
www.resprod.com
In my opinion (and you did by this book
for my opinion) these are the only whole-
house humidifiers to use.

Programmable Thermostats:
White-Rodgers Company
9797 Reavis Rd.
St Louis, MO 63123
(888) 725-979
www.white-rodgers.com
Very good programmable thermostats,
I use them all the time. They are worry
free and trouble free.

*The publisher has made every effort to produce
accurate information at the time of printing.
For up to date information please consult Lou
Manfredini Recommended Products at Ourhouse.com*

Glossary

blistering: a bump in cement that looks like a blister you get on your hand, only this one flakes away.

ceiling joist: a wooden or metal beam that spans across a ceiling, from wall to wall, to hold up the drywall or plaster.

circuit breaker: a device that calibrates how much electric current is flowing through the wires, and shuts down if it becomes overloaded.

chimney cap: a hat that covers the top of the flue pipe to keep rain, snow and animals from getting inside.

clean out door: a metal door that is usually at the base of your basement fireplace to remove cinders. It can also be found on the exterior of your home.

closet flange: the part of the plumbing waste pipe that helps secure the toilet bowl to the floor.

composite decking material: a product manufactured from recycled grocery bags and sawdust to form a wood-like material. It's cool!

condensing unit: that big fan thing outside your home. It runs the refrigerant through your air conditioner and then back outside to keep your home cool.

conduit: the metal pipe through which you thread the wires for your electrical system.

continuous ridge vents: a roof inlet that is installed on a roof's peak and runs across the entire length.

dedicated circuit: a circuit in your home designated to service only one appliance, such as a microwave, dishwasher, refrigerator or cold water heater.

drain tile: a pipe buried around your home to channel ground water into your sump pump or sewer system.

duct/duct work: this metal raceway carries the air in your forced air heating and air-conditioning system through your home.

ductless air-conditioning: an air-conditioning system that places a fan unit in a room and functions without any ductwork. The only holes you need to make in your walls are for the lines that carry the refrigerant to the fan unit.

ejector pump: the pump in your basement that carries waste from all below-grade plumbing pipes such as a basement toilet or a washing machine.

electrical panel: the cabinet that holds all the circuit breakers for your home.

electrostatic filter: a furnace filter that creates static to catch airborne dust coming through your furnace.

Glossary

epoxy: a type of glue that is extremely strong and water-tight.

exterior cladding: a coating that covers wood so you never have to paint.

flashing: a metal strip that joins the roof and the chimney or the roof and a wall, and protects from water seepage. Sometimes it's several pieces.

feather: to sand a ridge of paint so you do not see a line.

float ball: an older type of valve system that shuts off the water inside the toilet tank when it is full.

floating-cup ball cock: a valve system that shuts off the water in the toilet tank when it is full (a newer version of a float ball).

flue: the pipe that carries the spent gases from your furnace or cold water heater out through your chimney.

foundation vents: air inlets that are set into or just above the walls of your foundation to circulate air through the crawl space.

ground (grounded): a wire that bonds the electrical system.

ground fault circuit interrupter (GFCI): a mini circuit breaker within an electrical outlet. If there is a short, it will immediately shut down the electricity feeding to the outlet.

hose bib: the external water valve on your home.

humidifier: an appliance that adds moisture to the air in your home.

jamb: the two vertical sections of a door frame that attach to the hinges on one side and to the door latch on the other.

laminate: a plastic sheet that is bonded to wood to form a counter top or floor.

linoleum: a plastic flooring material that comes in sheets or squares.

load calculation: a formula that determines how much electricity you need to run your home.

main water valve: the valve that controls all the flow of water to your home.

mudjacking: a process where a grout solution is injected under a sagging concrete slab or stair to raise the structure back to its original state, also known as slabjacking.

mushroom vents: roof inlets that are installed on top of your roof to ventilate the attic space.

National Electric Code®: All homes in the United States must comply with these electrical standards, many cities have local codes with additional criteria.

Glossary

offset flange: a closet flange that allows you to move the toilet over about 2 inches.

overflow valve: a valve that releases water if temperature or pressure becomes too high (same as a pressure valve).

planing: to shave off a thin layer of wood from the side or top of a door.

pleated filter: a very high-density filter that traps more airborne dust than a conventional (cheap!) filter.

plumbing stack: the vertical pipes that comprise the main waste and vent pipes for your home's plumbing system.

pressure valve: a valve that releases water if temperature or pressure becomes too high (same as an overflow valve).

recessed light: a light fixture that is set into the ceiling.

register: an opening into a room that can control the flow of warm or cool air generated by your forced air heating or air-conditioning system.

remortise: a process by which you cut away wood to recess a hinge.

Romex®: a type of electrical wiring made of plastic-coated cable that runs through the walls to feed the electrical outlets in your home (it's like a heavy extension cord).

sash: the part of the window frame that goes up and down.

sheet good: a continuous piece of flooring that usually comes without seams.

sheeting: the plywood or lumber that is used under shingles.

short circuit: an interruption in electric current that can cause a circuit breaker to trip.

shower cartridge: the interior portion of the shower valve that regulates the water pressure and temperature.

shower valve: the portion of the shower faucet that controls water pressure and temperature.

slabjacking: a process where a grout solution is injected underneath a sagging concrete slab or stair to raise the structure back to its original state. Also known as mudjacking.

soffit vents: the inlet on the underside part of the roof that allows air to enter the roof space.

sone rating: the amount of noise a device makes, the lower the sone rating, the quieter the device.

space pack: a type of central air-conditioning system that is a cooling unit only and provides the cool air via flexible ductwork.

stranded wire: a type of electrical wire made up of many small wires twisted together.

stucco: a cement-based coating applied to the exterior of a home.

submersible switch: a switch that can be placed under water to control a sump pump motor.

sump pump: a pump that removes the water from a pit that collects ground water, rainwater or wastewater.

sump pump pit: a recessed cavity that holds the sump pump.

three-way switch: an electrical device that can control a light fixture from two different locations.

tuckpointing: a process where new mortar is installed in the joints of a masonry home.

two-wire connection: a wire connection that requires no third wire.

waste riser: the section of water pipes that run vertically and carry waste water from your shower, washing machine and dish washer, etc., to a sewer or septic tank.

wattage rating: the designation that tells you how much power (wattage) an electrical fixture can handle and, therefore, what size light bulb you can install.

wicking: to soak up like a sponge.

wood sleepers: the strips of wood under a finished floor that secure the floor.

wood windows: windows fabricated with wood frames.

vinyl windows: windows fabricated with vinyl frames.

zip tool: a tool used to remove vinyl siding from your home's exterior.